THE NATIONAL TRUST

Investigating

THE ROMANS

By Tim Copeland

Illustrated by Peter Stevenson

CONTENTS

Introduction

In AD43 the Roman Army was sent by the Emperor Claudius to invade Britain and to make it part of the Roman Empire. The army landed on the South Coast and began to make a new Roman province called Britannia which was to be part of the Empire for nearly 400 years.

Written evidence

The reason we know so much about a people who lived thousands of years ago is that they could write. In fact, the Romans were the first people to bring writing to Britain. From their words we can find out about how the country was conquered and what some aspects of everyday life were like.

Atlantic Ocean

BRITANNIA

GAUL

Rome

Mediterranean Sea

0   1000 km

One-sided stories

The Romans wrote histories of their conquests to be read by people in Rome. But they give us a one-sided story since the Celtic tribes did not write things down. The Romans always showed themselves to be brave and civilised. This is how Julius Caesar reported one battle:

'Our soldiers held out, and for more than four hours fought with utmost bravery, killing some of the enemy but suffering only a few wounds themselves. As soon as the cavalry came in sight, the enemy threw away their weapons and fled.'

The Roman Empire was at its greatest in the 2nd century. It stretched across Europe, along North Africa and into the Middle East.

Julius Caesar, *The Battle for Gaul*, translated by Anne and Peter Wiseman, Chatto and Windus, 1980

Tombstone tales

We can learn about ordinary people from writing carved on stones such as tombstones. These tell us how long people lived, what they did and where they came from – although not the date they died:

'To the spirits of the departed. Julius Valens, veteran of the II Legion Augusta. Lived 100 years. Julia Secundina, his wife and Julius Martinus, his son, had this made.'

'Julius Vitalis, Armourer of XX Legion Valeria Victrix, with 9 years service, aged 29, a Belgian, buried at the expense of the Guild of Armourers. Here he lies.'

Don't I look great!

Another way we can find out about the Romans is to read what's written on coins. They tell us about when the emperors reigned in Rome. The Emperor knew that the main way that people outside Rome would see him was on coins, so he made himself look really handsome and strong. On the back of the coin he put something that made him look good, such as a victory in battle, or he put an institution that he wanted to keep on his side, such as the army.

GAIUS VALERIUS AMANDUS' SALVE AFTER AN ATTACK OF EYE INFLAMMATION

GAIUS VALERIUS AMANDUS' VINEGAR OINTMENT FOR RUNNING EYES

GAIUS VALERIUS AMANDUS' MIXTURE FOR CLEARING THE VISION

Writing also tells us about people's jobs and other people's problems. Some small stones were inscribed for stamping on blocks of ointment and tell us that eye problems were common.

Writing on wax

The Romans wrote on tablets – small wooden boards covered in wax. They used a metal tool, called a *stylus*, which had a sharp end to scratch the wax and a blunt end for smoothing the wax down afterwards. The tablets were often burnt when they became worn.

Recently, at Vindolanda, a Roman fort near Hadrian's Wall in Northumberland, many tablets were found. The wet conditions had stopped the wood from decaying.

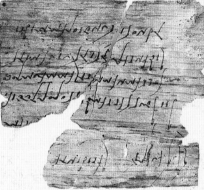

The tablets tell us a lot about everyday life in the fort and have lists of duties and foodstuffs. This letter sent to a soldier shows us that he needed the same sort of things as we do today:

'I have sent you pairs of socks, two pairs of sandals and two pairs of underpants. Greet your friends with whom I pray you live in the greatest good fortune.'

A.K. Bowman, *Life and Letters on the Roman Frontier*, 1994

Evidence in the earth

Archaeology is the study of things that have survived from a time in the past. These might be traces of buildings, fields or roads, or objects such as pots, jewellery or tools, or even things that were once living, like seeds, pollen or bones. They can tell us about life from that time. The Romans left lots of this evidence for us to study.

Accidental discovery

In the past Roman sites were often found by accident. The Roman villa at Chedworth was discovered in 1864 when a gamekeeper found pottery in the soil. The villa was then uncovered to find mosaic pavements and valuable objects.

NATIONAL TRUST

Victorian visitors at the newly-discovered villa site in Gloucestershire

An important type of archaeological evidence is from things that were once living. Even the tiniest pollen grains from flowers of plants and trees often survive in the soil on Roman sites. They tell us what the land around it was like or what was being grown.

How we investigate

Since surprise discoveries like Chedworth, archaeologists have invented planned ways of finding Roman sites:
● One way is to walk across ploughed fields and look for building materials, pottery and coins in the plough soil which give clues about where buried sites are.
● Another way is to look from the air. Crops growing over buried walls do not have long roots and are lighter in colour. If there are buried Roman ditches, crops can put down long roots to get more water and are often darker in colour.

Toilet tales!

Seeds or pips have been found in pits used for human waste. They give all sorts of clues about what people ate.

Using electricity to look underground

More can be discovered by using below-ground radar or by passing electric currents through the soil to find walls, pits and ditches. This does not damage the site. Archaeologists might then explore a site by digging into it carefully to find out more information such as:

- how old the site is
- how it was altered
- when it was abandoned
- what happened there
- whether it was a wealthy building

NATIONAL TRUST

Buried artefacts

Materials like wood, bone, cloth and leather, decay quickly and iron rusts away. But some materials can survive for a very long time such as stone and pottery, and metals like gold, silver or bronze. These artefacts tell us if a site belonged to somebody wealthy – through the quality of the material and the amount of decoration on objects.

> Artefacts can tell if a building was a home, farm, place of worship or industrial site. We can even guess what a room was used for by the artefacts found in it.

NATIONAL TRUST

Crop marks at Wroxeter Roman city, Shropshire

Reading the bones

There's nothing like human bones to give us information about people's lives – how old they were, what sex they were, and sometimes why they died. Teeth can give us clues to the person's diet and their age when they died. The way they are buried might tell us what their religion was.

Any objects buried with a body give us more hints. And let's not forget animal bones which help us to work out what species the Romans kept and so what meat they ate.

Who were the Celts?

The Celts were the people living in Britain when the Roman army invaded. During the time that Britain was part of the Roman Empire, most of the population were Celts. When Britain stopped being a part of the Roman Empire about AD410 most of the people were probably descendants of the Celts. The Celts had their own religion, art and way of life. After the Roman Conquest the Celtic way of life changed to be more like that of the Romans.

Do you think the Celts were really so backward?

Painted blue

Julius Caesar tells us about the Celts:

'Most of those who live in the middle of the island do not grow corn, but live instead on milk and meat and clothe themselves in skins. All Britons dye themselves with woad, which produces a blue colour, and as a result their appearance in battle is very frightening. They wear their hair long, shave all their bodies except their heads and upper lip. Wives are shared between groups of ten or twelve men.'

Julius Caesar, *The Battle for Gaul*, Chatto and Windus, 1980

A simple life?

Another writer says:

'Britain is inhabited by native tribes who live in old ways; they use chariots in war, and their houses are simple, built for the most part of reeds or logs. Their way of life is poor and far different from the luxury given by wealth'.

Looking for facts

The evidence tells us a very different story about the Celts. Remains show they lived in round houses with the timber roofs covered in straw thatch and the walls plastered with mud to make them waterproof. Inside, many of the houses had as much space as a modern three-bedroomed house! A fire inside kept them warm but it would have been very smoky as there were no windows.

Celtic homes were well insulated for cold winters. The Celts would probably have seen the Roman mosaic floors, which were made of stone, as being a strange idea in a cold climate, especially as a fire had to be lit in order to heat the air which kept the floors warm!

Celtic defences

Hillforts, such as Badbury Rings in Dorset, were important places for some Celtic tribes. Badbury was defended by two large banks and ditches, had a good view over the countryside and was a place to stay safe during war.

Here was the place where the chieftain showed off his power. There would also be a market and corn stores in the fort. But few people lived in hillforts in peace time, as they would have their farms and villages to live in and work on.

© DORSET COUNTY COUNCIL / S. WALLIS

Unlike the Romans, the Celts had some women rulers. Boudicca, queen of the Iceni tribe in Norfolk, led the revolt against the Romans in AD60. To avoid capture when the uprising failed, she poisoned herself.

Wise men

The Celts' priests, the Druids, handed down their sacred knowledge about the earth and the immortal gods, which they learned by heart by word of mouth. It took an amazing 20 years to train to be a Druid. The Celts saw them as judges and advisers to tribal rulers. A Roman writer, Strabo, called them 'the most just of men'. But the Romans did not like the Druids because of the power they had.

Snappy dressers

The Celts took great pleasure in their personal appearance. They wore brightly coloured clothes, often with checks and stripes. The men wore short linen tunics over trousers and the women long dresses of wool or linen. They loved richly decorated jewellery such as belt buckles and brooches.

Hairstyle was important and women wore their hair long. The men shaved their beards but grew long moustaches, and may have used lime on their hair to make it stiff and spiky and yellow or reddish.

NTPL / DAVID NOTON

Avebury in Wiltshire may have been a meeting place for the Druids

Who were the Romans?

The Roman Empire was huge in AD43. It stretched from France (which the Romans called Gaul) in the west to Syria in the east, and from North Africa to part of what is now Hungary. The Empire was a large area with one coinage where trade could take place without the threats of pirates or war.

This bronze brooch was found in the temple at Chedworth, Gloucestershire

Anyone in Britain who wanted to be a Roman had to abandon the Celtic way of life.

'Who wants to be a Roman?'

The Roman authorities were very clever as they allowed people from countries they had conquered to become citizens of the city of Rome. The Romans thought that their way of life was the best and wanted other peoples to share it. So, being Roman did not mean coming from Rome or even Italy. It meant being a Roman citizen from any part of the Empire.

There were many advantages to being a citizen, especially in the army and in getting government jobs. Eventually, there were Roman citizens who were British Celts and who called themselves Roman, too.

Plain clothes

Dress was an important part of being Roman. A tunic was worn, loose or belted at the waist. Men's tunics were short but women wore longer ones. The Romans preferred plain, unbleached garments, with a coloured band around the hem or sleeves. They thought these were more dignified than the colourful Celtic styles. Underneath the tunic men probably wore underpants and women linen or woollen briefs.

The price of beauty

Being a Roman woman meant having an elaborate hairstyle with tight curls on the forehead and a bun. Styles changed, often copying that of the empress.

Women were also expected to have soft skin. One recipe for a face pack recommends using ten eggs, two pounds of vetch (a bean-like plant), two pounds of skimmed barley, twelve narcissus bulbs, gum, pounded seeds and one and a half pounds of honey. This would have been expensive as well as messy!

Men also had to suffer as it was the fashion to be clean shaven at the time of the conquest. If a slave did not shave him, he would go to the barbers to be shaven with a sharp knife or rough razor. This could not have been pleasant and many men got cuts. One Roman 'plaster' to stop the bleeding was to use spider's webs with oil and vinegar. No wonder some men chose to have their hairs plucked out one by one!

Toga tangles

The toga was worn only by men who gained important jobs. This was a difficult garment to wear. It was made from a huge semi-circular piece of material 5.5m long and 2m across. It had to be placed over the left shoulder and arm, taken under the right arm, back over the left shoulder and then gathered and twisted in front to hold it.

Men who wore a heavy toga had to walk slowly. It was difficult to turn around. In Rome it was thought to be such a nuisance that emperors had to pass laws to make sure it was worn on important occasions!

Learning the language

Being Roman meant speaking Latin which was the official language of the Empire. If any Briton wanted a job in government he had to hire a language tutor. Clerks working in docks and offices had to use Latin to do deals. Sculptors and masons had to pick the language up quickly and learn to carve in superb Roman lettering. Many Celts would have spoken Latin at work and their native language at home.

Roads, roads and more roads

Experts reckon that about 10,000 miles of road were built during the time Britain was part of the Roman Empire, most in the 1st century. Many minor roads were built and even remote farms were only about 6 or 7 miles from a fine, well-made road. This was one of the Romans' greatest achievements. The main roads built by the Roman army were first used for supply and communications when they were invading an area, and afterwards for patrolling the land.

Roman roads were like our motorways – direct, and good for fast transport. Troops could march and materials be moved quickly. Once an area was conquered the main roads were also used for trade.

Sort of straight road building

Although the routes of Roman roads appear straight, they are in fact made up of a lot of connected straight sections, so over a long distance they actually curve. The reason for the straight sections is the *groma*, or cross-staff that surveyors used. It had four weights hanging from cross-sticks. These were used to line up with each other and to sight straight lines.

The surveyors worked from high point to high point so the road between the points was straight. The general direction these roads were travelling in may have been found by lighting fires at the ends of long stretches or using homing pigeons and observing their direction of flight.

How much further?

The Romans thought it was important to tell travellers how far they still had to go so they put milestones beside the road. If there was one every mile there would have been about 10,000! We only know where 110 are. One is kept in Tintagel Church in Cornwall. The inscription reads: *IMP C G VAL LIC LICIN, Emperor Caesar Galaria Valerius Licinanus Licinius*. It was probably erected during his reign AD308-324.

Cross-roads at Badbury Rings, Dorset

© DORSET COUNTY COUNCIL / S. WALLIS

Funny miles

Roman miles were different from ours, measured in paces, not feet:

1 Roman mile = 1,000 paces or 2,000 steps

This was easily counted on a road by a marching army.

1 Roman mile = 1,480 metres = 0.92 of a British mile

Here's a useful formula:

13 Roman miles = 12 British miles = 19 kilometres.

Which way to go?

The Roman army needed to know about the roads across a country so that they could choose the fastest route to a trouble-spot. Also messengers needed to know how far away the next change of horses was. So the Romans made road maps, or itineraries.

The information from one of the maps, The Antonine Itinerary, survives and lists 15 itineraries in Britain. It's very useful as it tells us the Roman names of places.

A place to rest

The main roads were used by officials on horseback to take messages and orders to the army around the country and to carry news back to London (Londinium) and on to Rome (Roma).

Along the road were places where horses could be changed and where it was possible to stay overnight. These hostels, or *mansiones*, were places to rest, bathe, eat, sleep and change horses. One of these was on Watling Street at Wall, in Staffordshire.

Here is a section of Itinerary II from Wall (called Letocetum by the Romans) in Staffordshire, to Wroxeter (called Viroconium) in Shropshire:

Letocetum (Wall) to Pennocrucium (Penkridge)	*12 miles*
Pennocrucium to Uxacona (Oakengates)	*12 miles*
Uxacona to Viroconium (Wroxeter)	*11 miles*

So Wall to Wroxeter was 35 Roman miles

Letocetum and Viroconium both had a *mansio* but Pennocrucium and Uxacona were probably just places where horses could be changed.

Life in the Roman army

The Roman army was so large and powerful that the emperors tried to keep it as far away from Rome as possible! But life was not easy for soldiers in the army.

Quoted in *Service in the Roman Army* by R.W. Dawes, 1989

'They complained about the hardness of the work and especially about building ramparts, digging ditches, collecting food, timber and firewood, and all the other camp tasks that are either necessary or invented to keep the men busy.'

Outside Hardknott fort there is a bath-house. Wood was burned to heat the water, so the baths were built at a distance to reduce the risk of fire. Nearby is also a parade ground which must have been chipped from the rock to make it flat.

Inside the Roman fort

Hardknott is a Roman fort in the Lake District and tells us a lot about how the army lived and worked. It is sited half way down an important pass through the mountains and was built to control the route. It was called Mediobogdum which means 'the fort in the middle of the bend' in the river which flows through the pass. It was built in about AD120 and was home to 500 soldiers from Yugoslavia.

Today you can see the foundations of the four gates and of the walls and corner towers, which defended the fort. Inside, you can see the foundations of the headquarters building (*Principia*), the house of the Prefect (*Praetorium*) and the granaries (*Horrae*) but what's left of where the soldiers lived – the barracks – are beneath the grass.

NATIONAL TRUST / R. MITCHELL

Aerial view of Hardknott Roman fort, Cumbria

The structure of a Roman army legion

80 soldiers = 1 century

6 centuries = 1 cohort

10 cohorts = 1 legion

A soldier's tasks...

A 'century' of 80 men lived in each barrack block and there were eight men in each barrack room. Every morning they would go out on parade and be given their duties.

As well as 20-mile route marches to keep fit and patrol the countryside, the soldiers' duties would have been:

● guard duty at one of the gates or the headquarters, or patrolling the walls

● making bread in the century's ovens

● cleaning the barracks or toilets

● cleaning their armour, or the centurion's armour

● helping to run the baths

● collecting and moving supplies of grain, food, fuel or clothes

In a workshop at Vindolanda Roman fort near Hadrian's Wall, there were 343 men working, including 12 shoemakers, 18 men building the bath-house, wagon-makers and plasterers. After a hard day's work a visit to the baths would be welcome!

Off sick?

We get an idea of what a soldier's life was like from this list found at Vindolanda.

First Cohort of the Tungarians (including 6 centurions)	752
Of who are absent:	
Guards of the Governor	46
At Coria (another fort)	337
At Londinium and other places	73
Total absentees (including 6 centurions)	456
Remainder present (including 1 centurion)	296
From these:	
Sick	15
Wounded	6
Inflamed eyes	10
Total	31
Remainder, fit for active service (including 1 centurion)	265

Less than half the regiment was at the fort!

...and other skills

Soldiers in the Roman army did more than just fight. Here are some of craftsmen who were excused everyday duties:

Surveyors, nurses, horse-shoers, stone masons, architects, pilots, shipwrights, weapon-makers, glaziers, water engineers, trumpet-makers, horn-makers, bow-makers, plumbers, blacksmiths, lye-burners, wood-cutters, charcoal-burners, butchers, hunters, priests, medical assistants, clerks to teach, clerks of the granaries, clerks in charge of savings, grooms, tanners.

Hadrian's Wall

According to the writers, *Scriptores Historiae Augustae*, 'Hadrian set out for Britain where he put many things to right and was the first to build a Wall, 80 miles in length, by which barbarians and Roman should be divided.' Hadrian arrived in AD122 and decided to mark the northern edge of the Empire in Britain. We think he probably designed the wall himself as he was interested in mathematics and architecture.

A strong boundary

The Emperor Hadrian was more concerned with making peace than war. The Celts of Scotland would not accept Roman rule so one way to keep the peace was to stop expanding the Roman Empire but make its boundaries stronger, to keep out these non-Roman tribes.

It was Roman soldiers who built the wall, as this inscription tells us:

'For the Emperor Caesar Titus Aelius Hadrianus Antoninus Augustus Pius, father of his country, the II Legion Augusta built this for 4,652 paces.'

Roman Britain: A sourcebook, by S. Ireland, Routledge, 1992

To work out how many Roman miles of wall were built by the legion, look back on page 11.

Building the wall

The wall was made of a 'sandwich' of two outer walls with a middle of stone rubble and mortar. Experts reckon that an amazing 30 million facing stones were quarried, transported, shaped and laid. When 50 metres of wall was reconstructed at Vindolanda in the 1970s, over 3,600 litres of water were needed a day, to mix the mortar! The wall follows the top of a ridge so water had to be transported uphill from the valley. No wonder Roman soldiers complained about the work!

Forts and milecastles

The wall had forts along its length and at every mile was what we now call a milecastle, a small fort *(see right)*. Between each of these were two turrets about half a kilometre apart, so they had a good view of the countryside.

Keeping a look-out

Milecastles had doors through the wall. This meant that a good watch could be kept on who was passing through. Behind the wall was a road that connected the forts, and a deep ditch to keep unauthorised people away.

Everyday settlements

Ordinary people lived in settlements around many of the forts along Hadrian's Wall, as at Housesteads. These settlements were called *vici*. This is where soldiers' slaves and servants lived. There would also have been traders and merchants who owned the shops, and taverns where soldiers spent the part of their pay that was given in coins.

Not everything that happened in the *vicus* was lawful, even though it was close to the fort. There is evidence that someone was making counterfeit coins in one of the buildings at Housesteads.

There may be a picture of Hadrian's Wall made in Roman times! In 1725 this small bronze cup decorated with coloured enamel was found in a well at Rudge, in Wiltshire. It shows a wall with towers and some of the forts are named. No one is sure whether this is a picture of Hadrian's Wall or what the cup was for. Was it a souvenir of a visit to the wall?

Ghostly goings-on

Something quite spooky was found under the floor of one building at Housesteads ...the remains of two skeletons. One was an older man with the point of a knife in his ribs. The other skeleton possibly belonged to a woman. By law all burials had to take place outside settlements so these hidden bones are suspicious. Was there a murder in the *vicus* that went undetected for 1,700 years?

The Granary at Housesteads fort on Hadrian's Wall, Northumberland

Life in the towns

The Romans thought that grouping people in and around towns was an important part of turning the Celtic tribes into peoples of the Roman Empire. Each of the conquered tribes of Britain had its own town so that it was able to govern itself. Wroxeter, in Shropshire, was a typical tribal town. Its Roman name was *Viroconium Cornoviorum*, (which means Viroconium of the Cornovii tribe).

Everything happens in the forum

At the centre of the town was the forum. This was a massive building and it filled an entire block. It had a row of shops at the front, four on each side of a grand entrance. Inside was a large paved courtyard which had life-sized statues of emperors. Here stalls could be set up on market day for the tribespeople from inside and outside the town, as well as merchants from Germany, Greece or North Africa who sold their goods.

Food was also sold. Around the three sides of the courtyard was a colonnade where more stalls could be set up.

The basilica

On the fourth side of the forum was the basilica, a large, tall hall. This is where two annually appointed magistrates held court. The governor of Britain would have held trials here when he visited the town. These trials took place within a special area of the hall. It would have been raised on a platform with railings around. A statue or painting of the Emperor would look down on the events.

At the back of the basilica were seven rooms from where the town and tribe were ruled. The large central room was a shrine which would have had a statue of the Emperor and perhaps one of the tribe's patron god or goddess.

The other rooms would have been used as a town council debating chamber, a strong room for the town's wealth and a room where important records were kept.

Big houses, small houses

Archaeologists have discovered that Viroconium grew into a busy and closely packed town which was set out on a planned grid of streets. Some of the shopkeepers' houses were narrow and long, with shops at the front and the accommodation for the family either over the shop or at the back.

More expensive houses were built around courtyards and had baths and dining rooms with mosaic pavements. Poorer people would have lived in simple wooden cottages on the edge of the town, or away from the streets.

Other important public buildings in Viroconium were the baths, which were very elaborate, a market for livestock and many temples to a wide range of gods and goddesses. Later, there may possibly have been a Christian church. There would also have been a *mansio* – a hotel where government officials could stay.

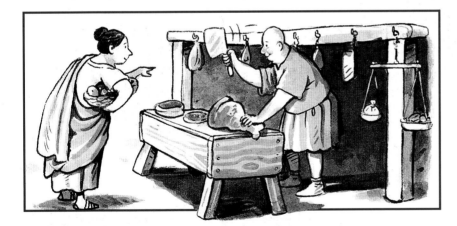

An aqueduct entered the town through the walls. It carried water for drinking, industry and the baths, in a V-shaped, clay-lined channel.

Impressive walls

Surrounding this settlement were walls with gates to the roads entering the town. The walls were meant not only for defence, but also to impress visitors with their size.

Walls also forced people to enter the town through its gates so that they would have to pay a toll on goods and livestock they were bringing in.

Relaxing at the baths

The baths were a very special part of life in Roman times, and everyone loved going. They were much more than just having a wash – more like having a Turkish bath or going to a leisure centre.

One schoolboy wrote in his exercise book:

'I must go and have a bath. Yes, it's time. I leave, I get myself some towels and follow my servant. I run and catch up with the others who are going to the baths and I say to them one and all, 'How are you? Have a good bath. Have a good supper'.

Quoted in *Britain in the Roman Empire* by J. Liversidge, Routledge and Kegan Paul, 1973

Coming clean the Roman way

The baths were heated by warm air travelling under the floor and through the walls from wood burning furnaces. The increasing heat made the bather's body sweat, which helped loosen dirt deeply ingrained in the skin. This would be removed with a metal scraper called a *strigil*. Oils and perfumes were then rubbed into the skin.

Hollow pipes in walls and ceiling carry hot air

The *tepidarium* or warm room

The *apodyterium*, a heated changing room

The *natatio* or outdoor pool

The *palaestra*, an open air courtyard for exercising

Taking turns

Men and women bathed separately, usually females in the morning and males in the afternoon and evening. The baths were usually only used in the daytime as they would have been difficult to light at night since their vaulted roofs were so high.

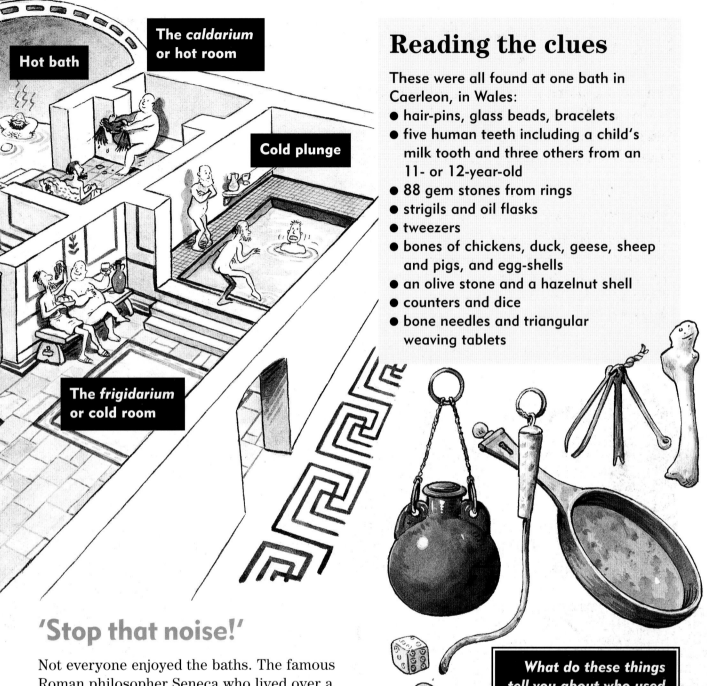

Hot bath

The *caldarium* or hot room

Cold plunge

The *frigidarium* or cold room

Reading the clues

These were all found at one bath in Caerleon, in Wales:

- hair-pins, glass beads, bracelets
- five human teeth including a child's milk tooth and three others from an 11- or 12-year-old
- 88 gem stones from rings
- strigils and oil flasks
- tweezers
- bones of chickens, duck, geese, sheep and pigs, and egg-shells
- an olive stone and a hazelnut shell
- counters and dice
- bone needles and triangular weaving tablets

What do these things tell you about who used the baths and what went on there?

'Stop that noise!'

Not everyone enjoyed the baths. The famous Roman philosopher Seneca who lived over a city baths complained about:

Panting and grunting of someone using weights for training; smacking noises of body massage; someone yelling out the scores of a ball game; commotion caused by a thief caught stealing; someone singing under the echoing vaults; someone splashing about in the public pool; shrill voices of hair pluckers advertising their trade – and worse, the yelling of their victims; incessant cries of the cake seller, sausage seller and candyman.

A Roman Emperor, Marcus Aurelius, agreed with Seneca:

'What is bathing? When you think of it – oil, sweat, filth, greasy water, everything disgusting!'

Marcus Aurelius, *Meditations*, translated by Maxwell Staniforth, Penguin Classics, 1975

Gods and goddesses

In Celtic and Roman religions it did not matter whether a person was good or bad as far as the gods were concerned. The gods or goddesses had nothing to do with a person's afterlife. The important thing was to make sure the god or goddess was on your side by sacrificing to them, sometimes their own special animal. In this way the deity would not punish you and might grant you your wishes.

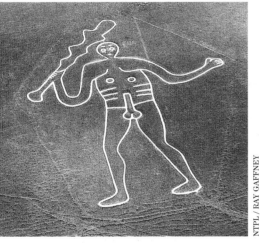

The Cerne Abbas giant in Dorset dates back to the 2nd century

NTPL / RAY GAFFNEY

Who was worshipped in Roman Britain?

The Romans had a large number of gods and goddesses. The most important were the three gods of Rome: Jupiter, Juno and Minerva. Jupiter was the sky god, but he was also the chief god of Rome and was called Jupiter Best and Greatest. He was the spirit of Rome itself. Juno shared Jupiter's importance over the other gods and was the main goddess of women. Minerva was a goddess of war, wisdom and crafts.

Mighty Hercules

Mars, god of war, and Mercury, messenger and god of traders, were very popular in Britain. Hercules was a well-known defender against evil. He is usually shown with a club in one hand and may be the figure cut into the chalk at Cerne Abbas. Other gods worshipped in Roman Britain include Silvanus a woodland god, Apollo the god of healing and the sun, Aesculapius (a healer) and Neptune, the sea god. Popular goddesses were Venus, Fortuna, Victory and Diana, the hunter.

Many mothers

There are many statues of Mother Goddesses. There are usually three figures, often holding babies, loaves of bread, fruit or fish. The number three was important to the Celts and some pictures of hooded dwarves appear in triplicate.

Household gods

The Romans believed that each place had a protecting god who had to be worshipped in order to bring good luck to the people who lived there. These were called *genii loci*, the spirits of the place, and so every house had its own altar to the household gods and they would be worshipped every day in the morning and at mealtimes.

Temples were generally very small and had a statue of the god or goddess, which was covered to keep the weather and birds off it. Sacrifices usually took place outside and afterwards people would enter the temple to talk to the deity. At some temples there were shops to buy sacrifices, chickens or small animals. People would travel a long way to worship the gods so there would be hostels and markets near temples.

For a time even the Roman emperors were worshipped as gods after they died. This temple to Claudius once stood at Colchester in Essex.

A nasty curse

Sometimes a worshipper wanted to get someone back for doing something to them! They would write a curse, a nasty request to a god, on a small piece of lead and pin it face down to a wall so only the god could see it. This one was found in London, where the woman must have done something dreadful:

'I curse Tretia Maria and her life and her mind and memory and liver and lungs mixed up together, and her words thoughts and memory; thus may she be unable to speak.'

Quoted in *Britain in the Roman Empire* by J. Liversidge, Routledge and Kegan Paul, 1973

A new religion

When Christianity arrived in the country around AD300, churches were built in some Roman towns. Christianity said that the way you lived decided what happened to you in your afterlife. It also taught that Jesus could help you get to heaven if you followed his teaching.

Because it was important that people should be together to hear the words of Jesus' followers, a church was often built like the basilica in the town, rather than the Roman temple which was a place to keep the statue dry and protected.

Life in the countryside

Most people in Britain lived in the countryside in Roman times. Some lived in houses that were copies of Roman houses in Italy which we call 'villas'. Many more people lived in villages or on simple farms.

Copying Rome

Villas were pretty smart buildings built of stone. They copied Roman architectural fashions – they were rectangular and often had baths and mosaic pavements. They even had under-floor heating systems called *hypocausts*. Some were very small, just a few rooms without mosaics or baths. Others were large, almost palaces, which belonged to very rich people.

Nearly all villas were on land that could be farmed and many were built from the money earned from farming. Some stone villas were built on the sites of Celtic roundhouses. From this we can guess that Celts who became wealthy wanted to be like the Romans.

A wealthy villa

Chedworth Roman Villa in Gloucestershire was a very rich building. Archaeologists have excavated the higher of the two courtyards found. This has two suites of baths, a dining-room and other rooms for accommodation.

Many of the rooms have colourful, detailed mosaics and the walls were once decorated in painted plaster. In the dining-room is a well-known mosaic showing the four seasons.

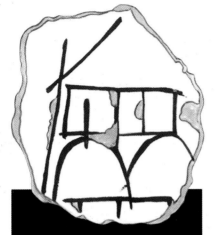

A tile found at a villa in Gloucestershire had this drawing scratched on it. It might be a doodle of the villa itself!

The mosaics and carved stone show us that Chedworth Roman Villa was a wealthy place. It may have been the country home of someone from the nearby town of Cirencester, known as Corinium. Some people think that the villa may have been a centre for religion because so many statues have been found and there is a huge temple nearby.

NTPL / IAN SHAW

Investigating the land

When archaeologists look carefully at the countryside around villas, they find traces of farms and villages where most of the Celtic people would have lived and worked. They also find traces of simple roundhouses where the farm workers would have lived.

In between the settlements the remains of fields can sometimes be seen from the air. Those of the Roman period are small squares, making a chessboard pattern. These fields were in use for a long time before the Romans arrived.

From pollen in the soil we can tell that Wales and western England had more woodland in the Roman period than we have today. But in central southern England, many places had less.

Keeping cows and making wine

Dug up bones and seeds tell us how the countryside was used. Cattle, sheep and pig bones were the most common in the Roman period. There are usually many more beef bones than the other two, and more sheep than pig. Other animals kept for meat include chicken, duck, geese and goats. Wheat and barley were their favourite cereals, though some oats and rye were grown. It seems the Romans even grew grapes to make wine as grape pips have been found in the soil.

23

Children in Roman Britain

In lots of ways childhood in the Roman period was very similar to that of today – if you were from a wealthy family. If your family was poor, your childhood would have been very short and at an early age you would have been working around the house or in the fields.

© CITY AND COUNTY MUSEUM, LINCOLN

Rattles and dolls

Toys were similar to some we have today. The baby in its basket or wooden cradle played with hinged pieces of wood or clappers, rattles with bells or jangling rings. Children would enjoy the noise produced by shaking pottery animals with pebbles inside them – pigs were especially popular. Dolls were made of wood, bone or baked clay and there were toys on wheels that could be pulled around.

Favourite pets

Part of a tombstone from Lincoln (*above*) shows a boy holding his pet hare.

A small bronze mouse was found in a child's grave in York and other tombstones show children with birds in their hands. Birds could be taught to talk as well as sing and were favourite pets in other parts of the Empire.

We think the Romans may have had cats and dogs as pets. The clue to this is footprints found on tiles which cats or dogs must have walked on while the tiles were wet.

Boys and girls played with tops and hoops. Games that children play today – blind man's buff, dart throwing, leap frog and hide and seek – were also popular.

Ball games were played at the baths or in villa gardens. *Trigon* was a game where three players stood in a triangle and threw balls to each other as fast as possible. There was also a fast game for several players where the children hit a light ball with the palm of their hands. *Harpastum* was a much rougher game that might have been like rugby.

Going to school

Education for boys and girls from wealthy families began at seven. This would either be at home with a tutor, or at school. Schools were often in small rooms, shops or corners of the forum. The pupils, both boys and girls, were attended by a slave when they went to school.

The only equipment was a chair for the master, and stools or benches for the pupils. Work began before dawn and lasted all day with a break for lunch. The summer holidays lasted from the end of July to mid-October. In the five years of primary school, children mainly learned reading, writing and arithmetic. Reading included lists of words that were difficult to pronounce. Prose or poetry would be dictated, learned by heart and then recited. Punishment could be harsh.

The children of the rich would have been looked after by the mother or a slave, until they were seven years old.

When a boy turned seven, the father would take charge, perhaps getting him to help with his trade. Girls stayed at home, to help around the house.

Children learned to write using a stylus on a wax writing tablet, or pen and ink on scrap pieces of parchment and papyrus.

While boys from rich families went on to secondary school, girls might have a home tutor. At the age of 12, some girls were married!

Counting on an abacus

Counting was done on fingers or using an abacus. This was divided into columns: units (I), fives (V), tens (X), fifties (L), hundreds (C), five hundreds (D) and thousands (M). The counters, or *calculi*, were made of glass, ivory or bone.

What made Roman maths very tricky was there was no place value like our hundreds, tens and units. So CCCLXV (365) was a longer number to write than DCLI (651) which is larger. This system made it impossible to put numbers of the same value above each other for adding.

Try this addition sum to see why the Romans used an abacus:

CCCLXV	365
DCLI +	651 +
MXVI	1,016

Roman food and drink

Apicius wrote a book called *The Art of Cooking* and it is the only cookery book that survives from Roman times. The cook book cannot have been meant for beginners as no quantities of the ingredients are given! The recipes are all for very well off Romans – it is unlikely that many people in Roman Britain ate like this.

Fish with everything!

All of these dishes needed *liquamen*, a very strong and bitter fish sauce. Here is one recipe for it:

'Take the intestines of tunny fish and its gills, juice, and blood, and add sufficient salt. Leave it in a pot for two months at the most. Then pierce the pot and the liquamen will flow out.'

Do you think a cook would do this today?

Dormice or snails…

An elaborate Roman dinner would have three main parts. The starters, called *gustum*, might be eggs prepared in various ways, vegetables (raw or cooked), herbs, lettuce, mushrooms, snails or dormice.

Here's a dormouse dish by Apicius:

'Stuff the dormice with minced pork, the minced meat of whole dormice, pounded with pepper, pine-kernels and liquamen. Sew up, place on a tile, put in oven, or cook, stuffed in a small oven.'

…brains and belly…

The main course, called the *primae mensae*, included roasted or boiled meat, poultry dishes, lobster or even a boar's head.

'Well empty a pig's stomach, clean it out with vinegar and salt and then wash with water and stuff with minced and pounded pork into which you mix three brains, raw eggs, pine-kernels and peppercorns, and blend with pepper herbs, liquamen and a little oil. Fill the stomach, leaving space so that it does not burst. Bind both ends together and boil in water… take out and hang up to smoke so that it colours. Then boil again until done, adding liquamen and wine and a little oil. Open with a knife, and serve.'

...and dessert

The sweet course was the *secundae mensae* which consisted of various kinds of cakes or fruit.

'Stone dates, and stuff with nuts, pine kernels, or ground pepper. Roll in salt, fry in cooked honey, and serve.'

After each course, guests washed their hands

As they dined, guests were entertained by poets, musicians and dancers

Most people in Roman Britain ate bread and porridge, fruit and vegetables. They drank beer and could enjoy oysters which were plentiful at the time.

Enjoying the feast

The dining-room was called the *triclinium* (tri- means three and refers to the three couches around the dining table). Slaves served from the fourth side. People reclined on each couch, eating with their right hand and resting their left arm on a cushion.

The guests brought two napkins to use when eating; one to wear around their necks and one to wipe their fingers on. They would have their shoes taken off by slaves and be given sandals. Prayers were said at the beginning of the meal and pieces of food were offered to the gods by burning them on a fire after the main course.

Rich Celts ate like this and drank wine to show how Roman they were

New foods and flavours

Seeds and bones found in excavations of Roman sites also tell us about food. Some of the new foods the Romans brought into Britain were:
- pheasant, peacock, fallow deer and guinea fowl
- vines, figs, mulberry, sweet chestnut, medlar and walnut
- parsley, borage, chervil, coriander, dill, thyme, mint, garlic, onion, rosemary, sage, fennel and radish
- cabbage, lettuce, turnip, endive and mallow

Quite a collection!

Trade and industry

Before the Roman invasion, a writer called Strabo listed some of the things that were produced in Britain by the Celts: grain and cattle, gold, silver and iron, cattle hides, slaves and dogs bred especially for hunting. After the Romans came, many more things were made, some of which were exported to other countries.

From the amount of Roman pottery found by archaeologists, you would think that the Romans were always smashing pots! Their pottery survives because the clay it was made from had been burned.

Mining for metals

The Romans needed the metals listed above by Strabo, to make coins. Soon after the army arrived, soldiers started to mine lead ore for its silver content.

Gold was another important metal to the Romans. When Wales was invaded, in about AD47, the army began mining for gold at Dolaucothi in Carmarthenshire. They dug rock from the surface and channelled water to help wash the gold from the rock.

The pottery trade

Cooking pots had to be tough and inexpensive. They were often made in bonfires, so were black and very coarse.

The Romans had their own basic version of a blender – they pushed small grits into the wet clay of mixing bowls, before they were fired, to help when grinding up food.

NATIONAL TRUST

Pottery from Chedworth Roman Villa

Pots that were used in the dining-room needed to look good so they were specially decorated. These were usually fired in kilns. Some pots were painted with patterns, others had the decoration stamped on. They might be scenes from everyday life or scenes from hunts or games.

Marvellous mosaics

Mosaics were the Roman fashion for decorating a house and to have one meant that you were adopting a Roman lifestyle. Mosaics were very expensive as they were time consuming to make, so having a mosaic indicated that you were rich. A customer was probably shown a design book to choose the shapes to go in a mosaic – perhaps a favourite god or animal.

Because archaeologists have found a number of similar mosaic designs, they think that there must have been famous workshops operating from places like Cirencester or Lincoln.

A mosaic was either made at a workshop and then taken to the building where it was flipped over and set in mortar, or it was made on the spot.

Woolly warmers and beer

Britain was famous across the Empire for its woollen industry. Emperor Diocletian made a list of prices to be charged for goods throughout the Empire in AD310. He mentioned:
- the *byrrus Britannicus*, a heavy woollen cloak with a hood, which was one of the best cloaks you could buy. (The winter figure of the Chedworth Roman Villa seasons mosaic is wearing one.)
- the *tapete Britannicum* which was a heavy woollen travelling rug to keep your legs warm in a coach or wagon.

The only other British item mentioned in the list is beer, which was twice as expensive as Egyptian beer and so twice as good!

Money, money, money!

Besides the large industries, there were also small businesses in the towns. There were jewellers, bronze-workers, blacksmiths, and furniture makers (who sometimes used a stone called shale).

What made both large and small industries tick was money – the coins that were produced by the Roman government made buying and selling much simpler. It also made paying taxes to the Government easier.

29

The end of Roman Britain

In AD380, Britain was still part of the Roman Empire. The people had changed their way of life after 300 years of being ruled by the Romans. But just fifty years later, the Roman army had gone and Britain was on its own, no longer part of the Empire.

Defending the Empire

In the last part of the 4th century the Roman Empire began to fall apart. Tribes from Northern Europe began to invade and the Romans had to defend their territory and especially Rome.

Towards the end of the Roman Empire there were several emperors ruling different parts of it at the same time. In AD406 there were no less than three emperors, Marcus, Gratian and Constantine III.

Many of the soldiers in Britain went across to Gaul, to fight for Emperor Constantine III. Britain, being an island on the edge of the Empire, was left to look after itself. Soon trade and other connections with the rest of the Roman world ceased. The soldiers who were left in Britain did not get paid, so they soon left the army.

Coin crisis

As connections with the Roman Empire were cut, no new coins arrived in Britain. This made life in the towns very difficult as trade depended on coinage. Many industries collapsed, especially the pottery trade that was so important to the Roman way of life. Without coins, taxes could not be collected and the public buildings – like the baths, the forum and basilica – could not be maintained. Towns were where the builders and mosaic-makers lived, who might repair buildings. But they were no longer trading. Roads were not repaired.

Without the wealth of trade, houses in the towns fell into disrepair as people left.

Evidence in the ground

Archaeologists excavating Roman towns have found thick layers of dark earth over the rubble of the buildings. This earth may have been made by the collapse of timber-framed buildings with clay walls.

Pollen found in this dark earth has identified plants that grow on waste ground. What may have happened is that as parts of the towns became derelict, the grass, herbs, and weeds took over. Soon, trees also grew on the sites.

Pirates and new invaders

For many years there had been raids on Britain from outside. The Picts, who had moved from Ireland to Scotland, attacked across Hadrian's Wall. Irish pirates attacked Wales. And Saxons from Germany, looking for land, began to settle in the eastern part of the country.

The Roman authorities tried to stop the Saxon invasions by building a string of forts along the east and south coast, commanded by the Count of the Saxon Shore. But by the middle of the 5th century these had all been abandoned.

Abandoned villas

In the countryside things also fell apart. Many villas were abandoned when their farm produce could no longer be sold in the towns. The rooms of some villas with luxurious mosaics were taken over for activities like metalworking.

Landowners probably let some of their agricultural land turn into grassland and grew only what was needed for themselves.

The Roman fort at Portchester, Hampshire, was built to repel Saxons

With the links between Britain and the Roman Empire cut, and with the growing number of Saxons settling in the country, Roman Britain had ended. Anglo-Saxon Britain had just begun.

Places to visit

Hypocaust pillars of the hot room at the baths of Chedworth Roman Villa, Gloucestershire

To find out more about what life was like in Britain under Roman rule, you can visit the following National Trust properties:

Ambleside Roman Fort, Cumbria
The foundations of two gates, corner towers and some central buildings.

Badbury Rings, Dorset
An unexcavated Iron Age hillfort with impressive defences.

Cerne Abbas Giant, Dorset
A huge figure cut in the chalk, possibly representing the god Hercules.

Chedworth Roman Villa, Gloucestershire
A famous site in the woods with two bath-houses and well-preserved mosaics, especially figures showing the seasons.

Dolaucothi Gold Mines, Carmarthenshire
Unique Roman goldmines and an exhibition centre showing mining techniques.

The National Curriculum

Investigating the Romans provides useful background information to support the study of the Romans at **Key Stage 2**.

Hadrian's Wall, Northumberland
Five miles of wall running west of Housesteads fort, with milecastles and wonderful scenery.

Hardknott Roman Fort, Cumbria
A most spectacularly sited fort, with well-preserved walls, gate towers, internal buildings and a parade ground.

Housesteads Roman Fort, Northumberland
On Hadrian's Wall and the most famous Roman fort in England with remains of toilets, a hospital, barracks, and headquarters buildings.

Segontium Roman Fort, Gwynedd
A fort that was in use for most of the Roman occupation, barracks, headquarters buildings, walls and strongroom.

Wall Roman Site, Staffordshire
The well preserved bath houses of the *mansio* on Watling Street.

Watling Street, Staffordshire
A short section of this important road near to Wall.

Wroxeter Roman City, Shropshire
The tallest piece of surviving building in Roman Britain with remains of the baths.

For a full list of National Trust properties, see *The National Trust Handbook*, available from National Trust shops and good bookshops.

First published in 2000 by National Trust (Enterprises) Ltd, 36 Queen Anne's Gate, London SW1H 9AS

Registered Charity No. 205846

© The National Trust 2000

ISBN 0 7078 0330 6

Designed by Gill Mouqué

Printed by Wing King Tong Ltd, Hong Kong